Viva Casals!

Viva Casals!

Sayings, stories and impressions of Pablo Casals

Compiled, edited and with a foreword by
Julian Lloyd Webber

\B^b\
Biteback Publishing

This edition published in Great Britain in 2025 by
Biteback Publishing Ltd, London
First published in Great Britain in 1985 by Robson Books Ltd
Copyright in this collection and foreword © 1985, 2025 Julian Lloyd Webber

Julian Lloyd Webber has asserted his right under the Copyright Designs and Patents Act
1988 to be identified as the editor of this work.

ISBN 978-1-78590-988-7

10 9 8 7 6 5 4 3 2 1

A CIP catalogue record for this book is available from the British Library.

Set in Adobe Caslon Pro

Printed and bound in Great Britain by
CPI Group (UK) Ltd, Croydon CR0 4YY

FSC
www.fsc.org
MIX
Paper | Supporting
responsible forestry
FSC® C013604

To all lovers of the cello throughout the world

'I began the custom of concluding my concerts with the melody of an old Catalan carol, the "Song of the Birds". It is a tale of the Nativity; how beautiful and tender is that tale, with its reverence for life and for man, the noblest expression of life! In the Catalan carol it is the eagles and the sparrows, the nightingales and the little wrens who sing a welcome to the infant, singing of him as a flower that will delight the earth with its sweet scent.'

PABLO CASALS

Contents

Foreword
by Julian Lloyd Webber

Every generation has its brilliant virtuosi – play-ers who, by a common consent, stand that little bit apart from their contemporaries. And, just occasionally, another, greater, phenomenon appears: an artist so very special that he creates an entirely new horizon for his art, an entirely new approach to his instrument. Such an artist was Pablo Casals.

There is no cellist today who has not, in some way, been touched by Casals: his innovations wrought a revolution and changed for ever the accepted limita-tions of playing the cello; his teachings stand like a beacon, proud and resolute, for the rest of us to follow.

Such a magnificent upheaval was sure to cause dis-ruption. When Casals first began to include complete

Bach Suites in his programmes, other cellists were at first bewildered, then bothered, by his free interpretations. Yet Casals's love and devotion to the cello were so overwhelming that even his stoutest critics were forced, in the end, to acknowledge the arrival of a player destined to change the course of music for ever.

I am trying to resist the temptation to comment on the 'stories' themselves, to single one or two out, even if some are, undoubtedly, more significant than others. But the account of Casals's meeting with the theologist Albert Schweitzer indicates so clearly the cellist's need to enter the political arena that I must allow one exception. During a conversation with Casals on the role of the artist as a public figure, Schweitzer observed: 'It is better to create than to protest.'

'Why not do both?' asked Casals. 'Why not create *and* protest – do both?'

Casals's courageous stand against the fascists who had overrun his beloved Catalonia earned him the respect and attention of the world's most renowned leaders – from Presidents of the United States to the Secretary-General of the United Nations.

Here, then, is a portrait of Pablo Casals – in his own words and the words of others. Hopefully, no side of the argument has been left out. It's all 'in there': the love of humanity, the wisdom, the idealism, the courage, the obstinacy, the inspiration and above all – shining through the pages like a rare and precious jewel – the overwhelming, triumphant and *towering* genius of Pablo Casals.

Full of wit, wisdom and faith in the innate goodness of mankind, *Viva Casals!* celebrates a great musician who transcended his art to become a world states-man. Revisiting these stories 150 years after Casals's birth is inspiring, humbling and a timely reminder of the necessity to care in the face of inhumanity.

Julian Lloyd Webber
September 2025

Key life events

1876	Born in El Vendrell, Catalonia, Spain
1888	Attends the Municipal School of Music in Barcelona, studying under José García
1890	Discovers Bach's *Six Suites for Violoncello Solo*
1893	Studies at the Royal Conservatory in Madrid
1894	Begins touring Spain
1899	Debuts in Paris and London
1901	Undertakes his first tour of the United States
1903	Starts a lengthy tour of South America
1904	Makes his Carnegie Hall debut and gives a concert at the White House
1906	Forms a longstanding trio with pianist Alfred Cortot and violinist Jacques Thibaud
1913	Acquires a cello made by Matteo Goffriller, which he plays for the next fifty years

1914   Marries American singer Susan Metcalfe

1915   Makes his first recordings for the Columbia record label

1919   Founds L'Orquestra Pau Casals in Barcelona

1933   Refuses to perform in Nazi Germany

1936   Begins recording Bach's Cello Suites

1939   Flees the Spanish Civil War and lives in exile in Prades, France

1946   Refuses to perform in protest against the Allies' inaction on General Franco's regime

1950   Returns to public performance at the first Prades Festival

1957   Marries his twenty-year-old student, Marta Montañez

1958   Establishes the Puerto Rico Symphony Orchestra

1961   Plays at the White House for President John F. Kennedy

1963   Awarded the Presidential Medal of Freedom by President Kennedy

1971   Presented with the United Nations Peace Medal

1973   Dies aged ninety-six in San Juan, Puerto Rico

In concert

'I only heard Casals once, but as long as I live I shall remember the sight of that homely, almost dumpy little figure – more like a village organist than an internationally renowned soloist; as long as I live I shall remember the atmosphere created around him, the uncanny hush as six thousand or more people in the Albert Hall seemed to hold their breath for the entire duration of the Bach Sarabande he played as an encore.' – Antony Hopkins, writer and broadcaster

* * *

Ivor Newton, the renowned pianist, wrote: 'He sits with his eyes closed and head slightly to one side ("as though," an irreverent observer put it, "he didn't like the smell of his cello") in a state of almost exhausting concentration.'

* * *

'Casals performs', remarked one observer, 'with an arrogant impersonality.'

* * *

After a particularly moving performance, Queen Elisabeth of Belgium was heard to ask: 'Mr Casals, can you tell me, are we in heaven or still on earth?'
 Softly he replied: 'On an earth that is… harmonised.'

* * *

'At one of my trio concerts with [Fritz] Kreisler and Casals,' wrote the pianist Harold Bauer:

I noticed a man with a peculiarly inexpressive countenance sitting on my immediate left. He neither applauded nor gave the least sign of approval throughout the evening; I did notice, however, that his eyes wandered occasionally from Kreisler to Casals and then back to me. The programme ended with the Mendelssohn D minor Trio, where the coda begins with an impassioned lyrical outburst from the cello. My man took his hands from his knees, where they had rested the whole evening. He gently tapped his neighbour on the shoulder, and I heard him whisper hoarsely: 'I suppose *that* one will be Casals?'

* * *

Before a concert at his festival in Prades, Casals said to his duo partner, the Swiss-born pianist Alfred Cortot: 'You've always chosen such perfect tempi. It's as if you had a metronome set by Beethoven inside you. Young pianists today play much too fast. Do you realise that our total age is 163? Let's go out there and teach them a lesson.'

* * *

An extraordinary incident involving a public rehearsal

of Dvořák's Concerto in Paris resulted in Casals being issued with a writ for breach of contract.

Scheduled to perform with the conductor Gabriel Pierné, he arrived at the hall to go through the work and was somewhat disconcerted to find Pierné apparently completely uninterested in their discussion. Suddenly the conductor threw the score on the floor, exclaiming: 'This is a ghastly piece of music! It isn't worth playing – it's not music at all.' Casals could hardly believe his ears, and he reminded Pierné that Brahms had also considered it a masterpiece. 'Well, Brahms was another one,' Pierné screamed, adding: 'And you should be enough of a musician to know how awful the work is!'

The row grew more and more heated until word came to the dressing room that the audience was becoming angry at the delay. Casals insisted that he had no intention of performing the concerto with a conductor who felt like that about it – to do so would be a desecration. He not only would not but *could* not play it and was going on to the platform to tell the audience what had happened. But instead the dishevelled Pierné rushed on, shouting wildly: 'Ladies and gentlemen – Pablo Casals refuses to play for you today!'

Bedlam ensued as the audience crowded on to the platform. A distraught Casals caught sight of Debussy standing in the wings and quickly tried to explain the situation. Surely *he* would understand that no artist could perform under these circumstances?

To Casals's astonishment, Debussy merely shrugged his shoulders and said: 'Oh, if you really wanted to play, you could.' Casals assured the composer he could not, packed up his things and strode from the hall.

The next day he received a court summons alleging breach of contract and, although the prosecution themselves acknowledged there was a discrepancy between the requirements of artistry and the requirements of law, the judge ruled against Casals, fining him 3,000 francs.

Over fifty years later, Casals said: 'I would act the same way today. Either you believe in what you're doing or you do not. Music is something to be approached with integrity, not something to be turned on or off like tap water.'

* * *

The audience at a Casals recital in São Paulo remained blissfully unaware of the commotion which had been in progress only minutes before in the maestro's hotel bedroom. Rehearsing feverishly, both Casals and his pianist, Harold Bauer, lost all track of time until they suddenly realised there was less than ten minutes to go before they were due on stage. Years later, Bauer still remembered their dilemma:

> Off flew the day clothes and we pulled on our clean evening shirts in frantic haste. Black shoes: where were they? Collars, ties, studs, everything dashed into place with feverish speed. Into the box with Pablo's cello, have I got all the music, yes, let's be off. But Pablo still had his trousers to put on, and his trousers were rather tight. Setting his jaw and introducing his feet, he pulled violently. Cr-r-r-ack! The toe of his right shoe ripped right through the trouser leg, laying it open from the knee down.
>
> There was no time even for consternation over this hideous mischance. Ring the bell, rush to the door

and yell desperately: 'Chambermaid! Chambermaid! Hurry here, for God's sake! Come at once! Bring a needle and black thread! Hurry!' The girl came flying, and in three minutes Pablo's trouser leg was bound together again in a manner that would have done a sailmaker proud.

* * *

Cortot, reminiscing on his concerts with Casals and Jacques Thibaud, the French violinist, recalled what a great practical joker Thibaud was – usually at the expense of the other members of the trio:

One evening, in the artists' room, Thibaud found a castor which had come off his armchair. Just as we were going on to the platform, he slipped it down Casals's right-hand trouser pocket. Between the two trios Casals looked decidedly uncomfortable and, putting his hand into his pocket, pulled out the castor with a flourish.

Thibaud burst out laughing. Casals said nothing – but at our next concert I found it planted on me.

* * *

Casals's Viennese debut in 1910 began disastrously:

The Musikverein was packed – not a seat was vacant, but the first stroke I made with my bow went amiss and suddenly, with panic, I felt it slip from my fingers. I tried desperately to regain control of it, but my movement was too abrupt. The bow shot from my grasp and, as I watched in helpless horror, it sailed over the heads of the audience and landed several rows behind! There was not a sound in the hall. Someone retrieved the bow. It was handed with tender care from person to person still in utter silence. I followed its slow passage toward me with fascination and a strange thing happened; my nervousness completely vanished. When the bow reached me, I immediately began the concerto again and this time with absolute confidence. I think I have never played better than I did that night.

* * *

In America during the 1920s it was still the fashion for women to bring their fans to concerts, and they would flutter them continuously (much to Casals's irritation, being invariably out of time with the music). At one recital, a lady with a virtuoso fanning technique was sitting directly in his line of vision. Infuriated, Casals stopped playing to ask, as politely as he could, whether the lady might possibly refrain from her disturbing habit – whereupon she fainted.

* * *

On 9 March 1904, Casals gave the American premiere of Richard Strauss's *Don Quixote* and, as usual, arrived at the hall well before the concert to warm up in the artists' room. Strauss and his wife appeared shortly before the performance and Casals – anxious to check over some last-minute details – began work with the composer, only to be interrupted by Frau Strauss.

'Richard,' she whined, 'I'm cold. Go back to the

hotel and fetch my boa!' Strauss, who was authoritarian to almost everyone else, left without hesitation.

'I could have killed her!' fumed Casals.

* * *

'When I reach my bed after a concert I relive my performance like a nightmare… what it was like… what it *could* have been like. I go over the whole concert in my mind and hear again, with perfect exactitude, everything which went wrong, every single note. I cannot sleep until I have been through this nightmare.'

Concert nerves

'Throughout my career, nervousness and stage fright have never left me before playing. Do you realise that at each of the thousands of concerts I have played at, I feel as bad as I did the very first time?'

* * *

'It's no joke – this anxiety is a terrible thing. Every time I go on stage I get an awful pain in my chest. I say to myself: why should this be? But it is so. It is strange… one never gets over this condition, even at my age.' – Casals in his eighties

* * *

'Nobody can ever know the real meaning of nervousness until he has a great reputation to live up to.'

*   *   *

'I have never conquered that dreadful feeling of nervousness before a performance. I'm tormented. It is always an ordeal – the thought of a public performance is a nightmare.'

*   *   *

Lionel Tertis (one of the first viola players to achieve international fame) recalled: 'Just before going on stage to play the Haydn D major Concerto, Casals was in a terrible state of nerves. Suddenly he turned to me and, clasping both hands together, cried in a piteous voice, "Pray for me!" Needless to say, the performance was magnificent.'

On the cello

'The first cello I ever heard was played by José García, who was later to become my teacher. I was fascinated – I had never seen one before. From the moment I heard the first notes, I was overwhelmed. I felt as if I could not breathe. There was something so tender, so beautiful and human – yes, so very human – about the sound. I had never heard such a commanding sound before. A radiance filled me. When he had finished playing, I said to my father: "Father, that is the most wonderful instrument I have ever heard. *That* is what I want to play."

'And from that time, all those years ago, I was wedded to the cello.'

*   *   *

'The cello is like a beautiful woman who, instead of growing older, has grown younger with time: more slender, more supple, more graceful.'

*　*　*

Casals's love of the cello could be clouded by the long hours of technical drudgery he needed to devote to the instrument. Perhaps this might explain his immediate reaction to the mishap that nearly finished his career. One afternoon during his first American tour in 1901, he decided to climb Mount Tamalpais, just across the bay from San Francisco. Suddenly a huge boulder crashed down the mountainside, missed his head by inches and smashed onto his left hand.

'My friends were aghast. But when I looked at my mangled, bloody fingers my first thought was, "Thank God, I'll never have to play the cello again!"'

*　*　*

'My cello is a demanding tyrant.'

* * *

When asked why he always played with his eyes closed, Casals replied: 'I had to keep them open for a long time before I could risk closing them.'

* * *

'My cello is my oldest friend, my dearest friend.'

Early days

'My parents had very different views about my future. Only my mother felt I was destined to be a musician. They would argue constantly about this, and my dearest wish was to get them to agree. But how could I?'

*   *   *

'About the time I was fifteen or sixteen I almost committed suicide. I felt at loggerheads with a world where there was no justice, selfishness was rampant and charity non-existent. When I saw people walking peacefully in the streets, or going to their occupations, I thought: "How stupid they are to enjoy this miserable life!" I was desperately searching for a door through which I could find peace of mind. My mother showed incredible tact and sympathy, but my father could not understand me and did not realise how near I was to a fatal crisis.'

*   *   *

When Casals was eighteen, he left Spain to further his studies:

> The day after arriving in Belgium, I went for my first lesson at the conservatoire. I sat at the back of the cello class and listened to all the other students. To begin with I was very nervous, as the conservatoire had such a reputation for producing wonderful string players, but I soon relaxed because I was not too impressed with the standard. After all the other students had finished, my professor – who until then had given no sign of noticing my presence – pointed at me.
>
> 'So!' he said. 'You must be the little Spaniard the director has been telling me all about.' I said yes, but I did not like his tone.

'Well, little Spaniard,' he said, 'it seems you play the cello. Would you like to show us?' I said I'd be happy to.

'And what pieces do you play?' I said I played quite a few and every time he asked me if I played a certain work I said yes – because I did. Then he turned to the class and said: 'Well now, isn't that remarkable! It seems our little Spaniard can play everything. He really must be quite amazing!' The students all laughed, and by now I was angry with this man for his ridicule of me. I didn't say anything.

'Perhaps you will honour us by playing the *Souvenir de Spa*?' he asked sarcastically. 'I'm sure we'll hear something unbelievable from this young man who can play everything. But what will you use for an instrument?'

I had not brought my cello as I had expected only an interview. There was more laughter from the students. I became so furious I almost left at once. Then I thought, 'All right, they will hear me whether they want to or not,' and I snatched a cello from the nearest student and began to play. The room fell silent and when I finished there wasn't a sound. The professor looked at me with a strange expression on his face.

'Will you please come to my office?' he said in a very different tone from before. Together we walked from the room while the students sat quite still.

'Young man,' he said, 'I can tell you that you have a very special talent. If you study here and agree to be in my class, I can promise you that you will be awarded the First Prize of the conservatoire. It is hardly according to the rules that I should tell you this now – but I will give you my word.'

My anger was complete and I could hardly speak. 'You were rude to me, sir. You ridiculed me in front of your pupils. I do not wish to remain here one second longer.' The professor stood up, white-faced – and opened the door for me.

*   *   *

Casals was thirteen when Camille Saint-Saëns, the French composer and organist, arrived in Barcelona to give a recital. Afterwards, the great composer was invited to a friend's house to hear the young cellist. Saint-Saëns asked Casals whether he knew his A minor Concerto. Tentatively, Casals explained that he had only studied it on his own and had never heard it performed.

'That is the best possible way to learn a piece of music,' Saint-Saëns laughed, and proceeded to accompany Casals at the piano. Then he announced to the astonished listeners that it was the best performance of his concerto he had ever heard and, after embracing Casals like a lost son, sat the little boy on his lap for the rest of the evening.

* * *

'While I was studying in Madrid, I met the great violinist [Pablo de] Sarasate. He was an elegant gentleman, very debonair, with flowing black hair, a long, slender moustache and gleaming black eyes – and he smoked cigars incessantly. At one point during our conversation he offered me some brandy. When I declined, he exclaimed: "What? You intend to be an artist and you don't drink? *C'est impossible!*"'

* * *

'In my early days as a soloist I agreed to join a sextet at the fashionable Portuguese resort of Espinho so that I could make a little more money during the summer months. There were quite a number of important people on holiday there who became interested in the concerts, which were such a resounding success that I received an invitation to play for King Carlos and Queen Amélie at the Ajuda Palace in Lisbon. I left Espinho in such a hurry that I forgot to take my cello… so there I was – in the presence of Their Majesties – with no instrument! It was a very embarrassing situation! I had to excuse myself and postpone the concert until the next day.'

* * *

In 1893, when Casals was sixteen, he was introduced to the wealthy and influential Spanish nobleman Count de Morphy. De Morphy – impressed by the young cellist – wrote Casals a letter of introduction to the legendary conductor Charles Lamoureux, whose

Sunday afternoon orchestral concerts in Paris were among the most famous of the day. If Lamoureux decided to include Casals in his series, the young Spaniard would surely be on the way to an international career.

However, the conductor's volatile temperament was as fabled as his orchestra. When an office boy knocked on his door, while he was studying the score of *Tristan and Isolde*, and relayed the information that a young man was standing outside with a letter of introduction, he swore venomously. Rising to confront Casals, he complained that he was continually being interrupted in order to read letters of recommendation praising the 'unique' talent of the bearer. Without losing his composure, Casals said quietly that he had merely come to deliver a letter which had been entrusted to him – and he immediately turned to leave. This dignified behaviour evidently impressed Lamoureux, who emerged from his studio to call Casals back, whereupon he read the count's letter and instructed Casals to return the next day with his cello and a pianist. The following morning Casals arrived with a thoroughly nervous pianist to find Lamoureux complaining, once again, about the interruption. Not wishing for a repetition of the previous day's encounter, Casals announced that he had no wish to intrude and would be leaving at once. 'Young man,' Lamoureux snapped, 'I like you. Play!'

The maestro returned to his *Tristan and Isolde* while Casals began Lalo's Concerto. Slowly, the conductor, crippled with rheumatism, rose to his feet and remained standing throughout the concerto. When the young cellist had finished, Lamoureux embraced him with tears in his eyes.

'*Mon petit, tu es prédestiné.*'

It was the beginning of Casals's international career.

* * *

A year after the fateful meeting with Lamoureux, Casals attended a recital by Ignacy Jan Paderewski, the pianist and later Prime Minister of Poland, in the Salle Érard with Mrs Abel Ram – an Englishwoman of considerable means who gave regular 'musical evenings' at her charming home.

They found themselves sitting in the front row, and the longer the concert went on, the more the great pianist appeared to stare directly at Casals who, by now, was feeling distinctly ill at ease. Finally, he convinced himself that Paderewski must have spotted his old friend Mrs Ram.

Later, in the artists' room, Casals stood aside as Mrs Ram greeted the soloist, but Paderewski was not to be deterred. Fixing Casals with a penetrating gaze he announced: 'I already know this young man. Tonight I played for him. This youth is *prédestiné*' – exactly the same word used by Lamoureux the year before.

Ten years later, Paderewski heard Casals playing in Montreux. He greeted him with one word: 'Master.' Yet the two men performed together only once – in 1916, after which they never met again.

On his mother

'A mother, by nature, is something wonderful, but my mother must be placed on a different plane. To be a good mother is not the same as being an exceptional mother. I do not know of any other woman like her – and I have known many mothers through all of my life. Each word she uttered made profound sense because of her intelligence, her intuition, her nature.

'She knew about everything – music, medicine, architecture, agriculture – not only because she studied but also because, above everything, she understood. Perhaps what was most admirable about her was her high moral standard. She was ahead of her time and, moreover, she was so noble and so beautiful.

Important persons who came into contact with her saw in her an extraordinary personality.'

* * *

'If it hadn't been for my mother's conviction and determination that music was my destiny, it is quite conceivable I'd have become a carpenter. But I do not think I would have made a very good one.'

* * *

When Casals was fourteen, his mother refused to take him to London in order to launch his career. Doña Pilar Casals never explained the reasons for her decision and she certainly could have had no first-hand experience of the anguish and suffering endured by many sensitive adolescents who began their careers as 'infant prodigies'. The decision of this remarkably strong-willed woman seems to have been governed by her fundamental belief in life's destiny – that what must be, will be, but in its own time.

Many years later, Casals might well have been re-flecting the mind of his mother more than he knew when he stated: 'Only the mediocre are impatient – the great know how to wait.'

* * *

In 1895, with next to no money, Casals and his mother made their way to Paris in an effort to find him work. He eventually managed to get a job in the pit band of one of the less salubrious vaudeville theatres, the Champs-Élysées. Winter came early that year, and to make matters worse, Pablo contracted dysentery, quickly followed by enteritis, making him too sick even to play.

Years later, Casals would sadly recall the sacrifices his mother made for him:

One day when she came home and I was lying sick in bed, I hardly recognised her and I realised some-thing extraordinary had happened. As I looked in astonishment and dismay, I saw that her beautiful, long black hair had become ragged and short. I was sick at heart. She had even sold her hair to get a few extra francs for us.

She laughed about it. 'Never mind,' she smiled, 'don't think about it. It is only hair, and hair grows again.'

* * *

Casals's wealthy patron, Count de Morphy, would have preferred his protégé to have become a composer, but he underestimated Doña Pilar's resolve: 'With Pablo the cello comes before everything else. If his future is as a composer, then *that* can come later.'

* * *

'My mother was a genius.'

Other musicians on Casals

'Though Richard Strauss has made us think of Don Quixote as a cello, there is nothing of Don Quixote in Casals's appearance, and, at first glance, the plump, short figure with the bald head and the apparently inextinguishable pipe might, in its utter lack of romance, suggest Sancho Panza. But once he begins to play, anyone with the least perception realises his utter absorption in the music, his air of monastic austerity and his unswerving fidelity to the composer.' – Ivor Newton

*   *   *

'On March 18th,' wrote the English conductor Sir Henry Wood in 1911:

Casals made his acquaintance with the Queen's Hall Orchestra and myself. His is an interesting, if somewhat curious, personality. There is no outward show of virtuosity to attract the public, yet his technique, tone and musicianship positively command attention with the first stroke of his bow.

At this concert he played what is to my mind the finest of all cello concertos – Dvořák's in B minor. As usual, I used my own orchestral parts and whenever the solo cello entered, I reduced the accompaniments to a double quartet of strings and two basses. I found this worked admirably because there was no danger of swamping the soloist – so easily done owing to the depth of the cello's register. Any conductor who has accompanied Casals knows how fidgety he can be over a concerto. He has a habit at rehearsals of turning round to the orchestra and hissing them down if they dare to make too strong a crescendo, but I flatter myself I have always given Casals entire satisfaction. Before he arrives, I always make a little speech to the orchestra: 'Now, gentlemen! Casals will be with us in a few minutes. You know what an intensely light orchestral accompaniment he demands – no colour at all. So I beg of you strings to try and play on one hair of your bow; perhaps two – sometimes three – but never more. Thus you will save endless stoppages and many scowlings and hisses.' This always has the right effect and I think I am pretty safe in saying that I am the only conductor in the world with whom Casals has risked playing the Boccherini Concerto without a rehearsal.

* * *

Gerald Moore – Casals's pianist for several memorable recitals – found that words failed him when trying to describe Casals's unique talent. However, some twenty-five years later, he did attempt to explain something of the phenomenon:

Many a good musician of modesty unconsciously thrusts himself between the composer and the listener through his concern over his fourth finger, through technical insecurity or through fright… Casals had no such problems. Casals began where lesser mortals left off: supremely sure of himself technically, he thought only of the music – of the message of the composer and that he was the bringer of that message. I know this sounds trite, but with Pablo Casals it is literally true... an attitude of mind, of spirit.

For their first rehearsal, Casals asked Gerald Moore to bring Beethoven's last Cello Sonata (in D major, Opus 102, No. 2). The sonata begins with a fiery *allegro con brio* followed by a deceptively easy-looking slow movement, marked *adagio con molto sentimento d'affetto*, and the work is completed by a fiendishly difficult fugue.

'Casals indicated we should begin our rehearsal with the slow movement,' Moore recalled.

This has a slow noble theme with the most delicate dynamic inflections rising and falling within the phrase, which each player observes in like degree. If one player augments or decreases more than the other, the music is thrown out of proportion and becomes meaningless. Casals sang on his cello, and I crouched over my keyboard with every nerve alert and my very soul in my fingertips. We played together without exchanging a word for about two dozen measures. Then Casals stopped abruptly, placed the cello gently on its side, looked straight at me and said: 'I am very happy.'

* * *

Accompanied by Gerald Moore, Dietrich Fischer-Dieskau sang at Prades and greatly impressed Casals, who later said he had not been so moved by a singer since Julius Messchaert. However, at dinner after the concert, Casals spoke so much about humility that Fischer-Dieskau asked Moore: 'Does he feel that I'm conceited?'

* * *

During a performance of Brahms's G minor Piano Quartet, Harold Bauer realised that he had taken the wrong tempo and could only pray that Casals would follow. But Casals came in at his usual speed, throwing Bauer into confusion. Back in the artists' room Casals embraced Bauer.

'Please forgive me, Harold. I tried to follow you, but I could not. *C'etait plus fort que moi*, my fingers and my bow would not respond at that tempo.'

Bauer thought Casals, like Martin Luther, could not compromise, even when he tried.

* * *

'One never thought Casals was playing the cello; he was playing music.' – Paul Tortelier, French cellist and composer

* * *

'Casals was not only a unique cellist, a unique artist. He was also the sort of person I think Bach must have been: a complete man whose life and art formed a whole.' – Paul Tortelier

* * *

'The music that came out of his cello was the ideal. His sonority was unique. How can I express it? I somehow associate it with a fruit. It had a quality that was mild and yet with a touch of lemon. It was like a mixture of all the best fruits: juicy, yet not too sweet. I'm sorry to make a gastronomic comparison, but it is, I suppose, as good as any other. Casals's sonority was really indefinable; it was something spiritual. It so fitted the music that the sonority didn't seem important in itself.' – Paul Tortelier

*   *   *

After the 1961 Prades Festival, the great violinist David Oistrakh wrote to his son, Igor: 'Casals is an extraordinary personality. He plays with youthful verve, the intonation is incredible, the mastery unique, the power of expression in his performance moves one to tears.'

*   *   *

David Popper – doyen of the previous generation of cellists and a prolific composer for the instrument – heard Casals only once, in Budapest in 1912. His pupil (and later biographer) Stephen De'ak observed the elder cellist's reactions closely:

> His serious appraisal of the performance showed in the expression of his face, and he applauded after each piece. But a slight puzzlement veiled the otherwise interested countenance.
>
> Following the concert we did not attempt to go backstage to congratulate Casals. It was impossible to reach the artists' room because the entrance was blocked by hundreds of autograph seekers.
>
> We took the subway to Popper's home, and I was grateful for the noise, which prevented conversation. However, I managed to catch some general comments such as 'beautiful tone', 'excellent technique', 'fine musicianship' and 'splendid intonation'. Then, finally, as we reached our destination Popper said: '… Yet, in spite of all these things, he did not touch my heart.'

* * *

'One of the greatest problems of cello playing', said

Sir John Barbirolli, the cellist and renowned conductor, 'is the enormous distance you have to travel with your hands. Casals had a command of the instrument that had never been known before... a command which almost annihilated distance.'

* * *

In 1969, Barbirolli – who, although only in his sixties, already appeared considerably more fragile than Casals – visited Puerto Rico to conduct Sibelius's Fifth Symphony and Mahler's Fourth at the Festival Casals in San Juan. Casals's welcoming embrace was so powerful that a lens in Barbirolli's reading glasses, which hung by a cord round his neck, shattered.

'I'll never have them fixed!' said Barbirolli with delight.

* * *

In a letter to his wife after hearing Casals in Moscow, the violinist Eugène Ysaÿe wrote:

Casals is really a sensitive, profound artist, musical in the broadest sense of the word. No detail escapes him, everything is focused with tact, wisdom and discernment, and always without 'pose', without head movements. His body moves well; the action is the movement of the thought behind it and it is right, alive – full of emotion to the very depths of the soul…

* * *

The violinist Fritz Kreisler simply hailed Casals as 'the monarch of the bow'.

* * *

Harold Bauer recalled the time he sight-read through Brahms's F major Sonata with Casals:

As I started the second movement marked *allegro passionato*, Casals exclaimed, 'Why don't you play it at the proper tempo? That's much too slow!' I was surprised, and explained why, in my opinion, it should not be played any faster. Pablo looked over the piano part for several minutes and finally said, with a gesture of impatience, 'But of course! Let us begin again.' I never saw him more vexed. For once his famous intuition had betrayed him.

* * *

Ivor Newton wrote:

Casals never regarded his pianist merely as an accompanist – someone whose sole purpose was to provide a suitable background – but as a colleague taking an equal (if dynamically subdued!) share of the glory of performing a great work. At times it was even possible to forget what instrument he was playing, for there seemed to be nothing between us and the voice of the composer himself.

* * *

Milton Katims, principal viola of the NBC Symphony Orchestra, was often invited to Arturo Toscanini's home, the Villa Pauline at Riverdale – partly, he suspected, because he had a beautiful wife, Virginia, who also happened to be an excellent cellist.

Casals had been given a cine camera, and he asked Katims if he would film the great conductor relaxing at home. At his next invitation, Milton arrived at the villa armed with Casals's camera. Toscanini greeted the Katims and immediately became absorbed in a conversation with Virginia about obscure cello reper-toire. It seemed nobody could get a word in edgeways, but at last the couple paused for a moment's breath and Milton quickly put forward Casals's request. There was no answer from Toscanini. Katims repeat-ed the question – might he possibly take a short film? Still there was silence, so he decided to let the matter rest. When the time came to leave, Toscanini – always the most courteous of hosts – escorted the Katims to their car. Just as Milton was about to get in, Toscanini grabbed him by the sleeve and whispered: 'Casals thinks my Brahms too fast. No pictures.'

*   *   *

The Master of the Queen's Musick, Sir Arthur Bliss,

had a fascinating opportunity to observe Casals at work during rehearsals for a concert (by the Boston Symphony Orchestra under Pierre Monteux) which included his own *Colour Symphony*:

Casals was playing the Dvořák Concerto in the first half and was sitting in the stalls listening to Monteux at work on Debussy's *La Mer*. When the orchestra came to the short passage for divisi cellos in the first movement, Casals asked whether he might rehearse them alone for a few minutes during the interval. When the interval came, there was Casals leading the cellos through the passage, making suggestions as to bowings and fingerings, while other string players sat around eagerly listening.

*   *   *

The Hungarian-born American conductor Antal Doráti recalled visiting a Casals exhibition, which displayed all sorts of souvenirs and memorabilia connected with the cellist's life. 'Casals himself offered to be our guide and showed us the collection with exquisite, naïve charm. It was touching, and funny at the same time, to hear that serious, sometimes forbidding-looking man explain to us in deadly earnest, "These shoes I wore when I was three years old."'

* * *

After their 1945 recording of Elgar's Concerto, Sir Adrian Boult (then the chief conductor of the BBC Symphony Orchestra), who respected Casals enormously, was nevertheless moved to remark: 'There is no known conducting technique for keeping an orchestra together with this man. The only useful practise would be fly swatting.'

* * *

Recalling a performance he had given of Schumann's Concerto with Casals, German-born conductor Bruno Walter remembered 'not only his glorious playing but also his fantastic concentration on the technical problems of his instrument'.

Arriving at the Queen's Hall for the morning

rehearsal, Walter found Casals already practising in the soloist's room. Walter apologised, saying he had asked the orchestral management to let Casals know that he would not be needed until the second half of the rehearsal. Casals seemed quite unconcerned and continued with his practise. Later, he appeared on the platform and played 'with his characteristic seriousness and perfection', much to the delight of Walter and the orchestra. After the rehearsal, Walter returned to his room to change and heard the sound of Casals's cello wafting yet again from the adjoining soloist's room. That afternoon he went for his usual pre-concert stroll and, passing the hall, was astounded to hear 'that famous, noble sound' *still* floating from the artist's room. 'This', said Walter, 'gave me an impressive insight into the man's amazing absorption in his instrument. I listened to his intensive practising for fully fifteen minutes.'

As soon as the concert was over, Walter teased Casals for not starting to practise again immediately!

On the orchestra

'If I have been so happy up to now scratching away at a cello, how shall I feel when I can possess the greatest of all instruments – the orchestra!'

* * *

'Making music is what interests me, and what better instrument can there be than the orchestra… It is the supreme medium for anyone who feels music profoundly and wishes to translate the form and shape of his deepest and most intimate thoughts and emotions. And what appeals to me equally is the idea of co-operation. I am enchanted by the experience of many gathered together to make music.'

*   *   *

'An orchestra must be an institution of art, of light, of inspiration – not a machine for concert-making. The day this true point of view is comprehended is the day music will take its rightful place.' – From a letter to Adrian Boult, dated 12 December 1922

As a conductor

Casals's conducting career, which began with the Lamoureux Orchestra in 1908, extended over more than sixty years. In 1920, he founded L'Orquestra Pau Casals in Barcelona and conducted it until the outbreak of the Spanish Civil War. In 1923, Adrian Boult attended some of the orchestra's rehearsals:

> These rehearsals were really lessons… every member of the orchestra was made to feel the passage himself in its inevitable relation to the expression of the moment and the style of the whole work… We all know Casals's playing of the classics. Casals, the conductor, is no less great an artist.

* * *

One of the players in L'Orquestra Pau Casals remarked: 'Casals is not a conductor who shadow-boxes. All his gestures are for the orchestra. His sole concern is for the music and the interpretation of the composer's intentions. He sings… he inspires.'

* * *

In the middle of a rehearsal with the BBC Symphony Orchestra, Casals suddenly snatched the principal cellist's instrument away in order to demonstrate how a certain phrase should be played, but only succeeded in producing an awful grunt. To the great amusement of the orchestra, he dismissed the incident with the words: 'I'm not used to the cello.'

* * *

'We began our rehearsals with the first Brandenburg Concerto,' recounted Paul Tortelier. 'I shall never forget the depth of feeling he brought to the slow movement, with its poignant dialogue in D minor between oboe and violin. Performing that movement with Casals was unutterably moving. It was, I think, the most beautiful moment of my musical life.'

* * *

With his own orchestra (which he subsidised) Casals could have as much rehearsal time as he liked. Unfortunately, when it came to guest appearances with orchestras that had much tighter rehearsal schedules, the opinions of Casals's conducting would vary greatly. Bernard Shore, the principal viola of the BBC Symphony Orchestra during the 1930s, wrote:

> Unfortunately the orchestra often find it impossible to grasp what Casals is striving for, and at times wish to heaven he would demonstrate it on the cello. His stick would be reckoned efficient in an ordinary conductor, but it is inadequate to express that magnificent mind of his. Frequently it lets him down – being somewhat indefinite. When ensemble goes a little awry, he flaps both arms violently, but without sufficient grip to draw together the ragged ends. The stick is not always quite clear, and because of this the

orchestra is never perfectly confident, particularly at the beginning of movements and at changes of tempi. An orchestra needs something more than that the conductor himself should be inside the music.

* * *

'At that time [around 1928] the art of conducting completely defeated him', wrote Gerald Jackson, first flautist of the London Symphony Orchestra:

He was quite unable to convey his wishes to us in the matter of phrasing and he was unnecessarily finicky. His tempi, always so perfect when he was a soloist, seemed completely at sea when he had a baton in his hand. At one of his concerts we played the Brahms 'St Anthony Variations', and I believe this was even followed by a recording. When we reached the woodwind variation, before we could make the transition at the accustomed speed, we were so taken aback by his extraordinarily slow tempo that we stopped altogether with an involuntary, 'Oh!'

'So, gentlemen, why do you stop?' asked the visiting conductor. 'Brahms's *allegro* is not as anyone else's *allegro*.'

Some may call me a heretic for daring to impugn such a famed artist as Casals, but unfortunately I must record this as my experience; to me, then, he was no conductor, and I make no apology.

* * *

Yet Frank Miller, a cellist who played in the Boston Symphony Orchestra under both Casals and Toscanini said:

Casals, such a great musician both as cellist and conductor, would seek out the essential meaning of a work as did Toscanini, but each in his own way, for they were such different personalities. Like Toscanini, Casals tolerated nothing less than the complete revelation of the music's heart and soul and inspired the profoundest respect from the musicians who played under his direction.

*   *   *

According to Carl Flesch, the Hungarian violinist and teacher, when a Viennese orchestral musician was asked what Casals was about to conduct, he replied: 'I'm sure I don't know what *he's* going to conduct. *We* are going to play the "Pastoral" Symphony.'

Casals and the critics

Shortly after his first meeting with Casals, the pianist Artur Rubinstein was surprised to receive a visit from a critic who had just delivered a scathing review of his Parisian debut. 'Young man,' the critic began, 'I came to see you at the suggestion of Pablo Casals. This great artist – whom I hold in the highest esteem – has read my review of your debut here with great indignation. He said, "If you really think that well of *me*, then let me tell you that I believe Rubinstein is my equal, if not my superior."

'I must admit,' continued the uninvited guest, 'I was so impressed by what he told me that I decided I should get to know you better.'

* * *

'F. B.', a critic on the *Musical Times*, attacked Casals vehemently after he had conducted Brahms's 'St Anthony Variations' in London:

> Casals tried – and tried vainly – to get from the orchestra something like the sweetness of tone, the clearness of execution, which characterises his own performances. Had he used the time at his disposal in testing different tempi, his good taste would have told him that his own were hopelessly wrong. His misreadings of Brahms's 'St Anthony Variations' can only be explained by the fact that soloists in the green room do not know what is happening on the platform.

Casals, who was not known to pay undue attention to his critics, was furious – chiefly because he had been portrayed as living in a soloist's vacuum. The matter was debated for a while in London's musical press until the distinguished Arthur Fox-Strangways, former music critic of *The Times* and *The Observer* – and an acquaintance of Brahms – wrote an article proclaiming that Casals's tempi were exactly those of

Brahms himself. Casals was radiant with vindication yet, if mentioned, the incident would still upset him forty-five years later.

* * *

Casals's performance of Elgar's Concerto during the 1930s was damned, almost to a man, by the London music critics, yet when he recorded the work with Sir Adrian Boult in 1945 his interpretation was widely acclaimed. Sir Adrian was asked what the difference had been between the 1945 recording and Casals's earlier performance.

'None,' said Boult.

* * *

In his memoirs, Carl Flesch recalled a grotesque situation involving Casals and a certain Dutch music critic who, unfortunately, had gained most of his knowledge from reference books. For many years the critic had written for the *Nieuwe Rotterdamsche Courant* before being appointed to the *Amsterdamer*

Handelsblad, and it so happened that his change of newspaper coincided exactly with recitals Casals was giving in Rotterdam and Amsterdam. In Rotterdam, Casals was scheduled to play Bach's C minor Suite and in Amsterdam the G major but, as luck would have it, he was persuaded at the last moment to include the C minor Suite in both cities.

The critic's shortcomings were ruthlessly exposed, as his review in Amsterdam began with a high-minded comparison of the sombre key of C minor with the serene G major before proceeding to muse, at some length, upon the extraordinary differences in character between the corresponding movements of the two suites.

On Bach

'First comes Bach – then all the others.'

* * *

'Bach is for ever – and no one, *no one*, will ever reach the greatness, the profoundness and the diversity that is Bach.'

* * *

'I need Bach at the beginning of the day almost more than I need food and water.'

* * *

'The music of Bach is the perfect elixir of youth.'

*   *   *

'Then we stopped at an old music shop near the harbour and I began to browse through a bundle of musical scores.

'Suddenly I came upon a sheaf of pages, yellowed with age and crumbling to the touch. They were un-accompanied suites by Johann Sebastian Bach – for the cello *alone*! I looked at them with wonder: *Six Suites for Violoncello Solo*. What magic and mystery were hidden in those words? I had never heard of the existence of these suites; nobody – not even my teachers – had ever mentioned them to me. I forgot our reason for being at the shop. All I could do was stare at the mouldering pages and caress them. That scene has never grown dim. Even today, when I see the cover of that music, I am back again in the musty old shop with its faint smell of the sea.'

*   *   *

When Casals started to play the complete Bach Solo Suites in public (the first cellist ever to do so), he startled both audiences and critics alike. The incredulity of one renowned pedagogue was typical of his detractors: 'You mean he actually dares to perform those *studies* in public?' Other cellists, among them the distinguished German Hugo Becker, were outraged by his 'sacrilegious' approach to the music.

Although the disapproval of his colleagues upset Casals, he paid little attention to journalistic critics, especially as their opinions of his Bach playing tended to cancel each other out and certainly his audiences were thrilled by his 'free' interpretations.

'The purists are scandalised because I do that,' said Casals, referring to his staccato bowing in the courante of the Third Suite. 'Because it seems – it *seems* that in Bach's time staccato didn't exist.'

As was often the case, Casals's intuition proved to be right. Later research showed that both staccato and spiccato bowings were used by Tartini and Geminiani, and in *Traité de la Viole* (*Treatise of the Violin*), written as early as 1687, Jean Rousseau refers to 're-bounding bow strokes which are called ricochets'.

* * *

'The Suites had been considered academic works – technical, mechanical, without warmth. Imagine that! How could anyone think of them as being cold, when a whole radiance of space and poetry pours forth from them! They are the very essence of Bach, and Bach is the essence of music.'

* * *

By 1902, Casals would regularly include a complete Bach suite in his programmes. That autumn, while on tour with Casals in Spain, his pianist Harold Bauer had the opportunity to witness the innate Spanish response to great music. As he sat in the wings listening to Casals play Bach, he noticed a stagehand with tears streaming down his cheeks.

'The composer of that music must be Verdi,' announced the Spaniard.

'It is,' said Bauer, trying not to disappoint him, 'doesn't it say so in the programme?'

'I can't read,' said the stagehand, 'but I *know* it's Verdi. For Verdi is the only music that makes me weep.'

* * *

'I remember once a recital in Geneva; I was playing the sixth Bach Suite. All went well – the prelude, the allemande, the courante – until I came to the sarabande. It's a very difficult movement, with tortuous double stops, and just after I started it, my A string broke. I retired and changed the string while the audience waited. Returning to the platform I began from the very beginning. It's hard to play on a new string, but again things went well – until the sarabande: at the very same place, the new string broke!

'I put on my last spare string and returned to the stage; but this time I started playing a different suite. By then I knew that the Sixth Suite was not for me that day.'

* * *

In a BBC radio programme comparing recordings of the prelude from Bach's First Suite, Casals's interpretation seemed unique in its ability to let the music breathe. It was assumed this must be because Casals's performance was slower than all the others, so the different versions were subjected to the stopwatch – revealing Casals's to be almost the fastest.

* * *

'For the past eighty years I have started each day in the same manner. It is not a mechanical routine but something essential to my daily life. I go to the piano, and I play two preludes and fugues of Bach. I cannot think of doing otherwise. It is a sort of benediction on the house.'

* * *

'Starting the day by playing Schumann, Mozart, Schubert or even Beethoven is not good enough for me. It has to be Bach. If you were to ask me why, I should find it difficult to explain. I have to have perfection and serenity, and only Bach can inspire me with the absolute ideal of what is perfect and beautiful.'

* * *

'I have often said that Bach's music should be interpreted as freely as Chopin's, Schumann's and many other composers. It is because this rule has not always been observed that people have sometimes been able to say, "Bach is cold, monotonous… and boring"!'

* * *

By the time Casals reached his eighties he would simply say: 'Bach is my best friend.'

On other composers

'It is not necessary – fortunately – to play Bach, or to *be* Bach, all the time. All composers have different qualities, so why not take advantage of the fact and take pleasure from it?'

* * *

'Music has no barriers. Some will say Scarlatti was the only old master, others that Couperin was as great as Bach. Mozart and Beethoven speak an international language and one day we will be able to look back and see the whole of music as a continuous panorama of beauty.'

* * *

'Let us not forget that the greatest composers were also the greatest thieves. They stole from everyone and everywhere.'

* * *

'In my opinion, nothing that has ever been said – truly or falsely – about Beethoven can diminish the radiance such a mind has brought us. His music will always be looked upon as one of the most glorious gifts humanity has received.'

* * *

'It is possible to appreciate many works by great composers without *liking* them at all.'

* * *

'Mendelssohn is a romantic who felt at ease within the mould of classicism and who was able to solve, with innate elegance and imagination, the most difficult problems of form. I feel sure he will come into his own again.'

*   *   *

'Whatever people's opinion of David Popper, I will play his music as long as I play the cello, for no other composer wrote better for the instrument.'

*   *   *

When asked why many of Schumann's biographers hardly refer to the Cello Concerto, Casals replied: 'Because they have failed to realise its value. It is one of the greatest works one can hear; from beginning to end the music is sublime.'

*   *   *

Casals returned, years later, to a secluded part of the countryside which he had loved as a boy. The hazy, sun-drenched spell of Catalonia filled him with a blaze of enthusiasm and he heard himself murmuring one word again and again: 'Beethoven!'

* * *

'Bach and Beethoven exist all around us, and they will exist for as long as human beings are capable of feeling anything.'

* * *

'Ravel never showed any enthusiasm after a good performance! As soon as he became famous he lost all interest in performers and stopped going to their concerts. After knowing him as a young man, I could only feel a sort of pity when I discovered such aspects of his character.'

On modern music

'I have finally come to a definite conclusion: I will have nothing to do with what is called "contemporary music".'

* * *

'To my mind, "impressionism", of which Debussy and Ravel are the leaders, is a decadent deviation from the stream of great music.'

* * *

'Darius Milhaud has a great gift for composition and has given us some marvellous works. It is a pity he also thinks he should be "modern" at all costs.'

*   *   *

'The best composer of our times is Ernest Bloch.'

*   *   *

'The trend of music today, of the so-called "new" music, has put numerous composers of recent decades under a cloud. The promoters and experts of this movement claim that the music which we love and admire, above all the musical language that has been conceived and developed through the centuries, is no longer valid. This remains to be seen.

'However, it is clear that the noisy intrusion of this new trend, even if it has not injured the glory of the great masters, has had deplorable effects on the composers of the last few generations who have remained faithful to the very essence of musical art. The merits and virtues of "originality" and "innovation" have been trumpeted near and far, forgetting for the most part that originality is above all a natural gift and that innovations that express no feeling, that use an incomprehensible language and that finally lead to chaos, respond to no requirement of artistic creation.

'Composers, even great composers, who have refused to follow this road and have struggled to produce not "modern music" but simply "music", have almost disappeared from concert programmes and risk sinking into oblivion.'

* * *

'Music has to serve a purpose; it must be part of something larger than itself, part of humanity; and that is at the core of my argument with modern music – its lack of humanity.'

* * *

'The emphasis placed on originality leads to foolish aberrations. Each of us possesses as much originality as the most modest creation of nature. If you see a friend coming towards you in the distance, you will know him by his gait; he doesn't need to make fancy gestures in order for you to recognise him. Why? Because he has his own characteristics – his originality. In music it is easy to make gestures and write nonsense in order to appear original; the hard thing is to stamp one's own personality on a composition while using a comprehensible language.'

*   *   *

'Emánuel Moór, Donald Tovey and Julius Röntgen.* These are three very great composers still without recognition. But I feel sure their time will come.'

*   *   *

'It seems to me that Arthur Honegger is one of the contemporary composers of greatest musical value. In spite of his "modernism" he refrains from going beyond certain limits. He has been influenced by modern tendencies, but he knows how to select some

---

*   After hearing Casals's performance of Röntgen's Cello Sonata, Grieg wrote: 'This man does not perform, he resuscitates.'

innovations and not others, while remaining faithful to what we may define as the idea of music – something so many contemporary composers have just abandoned.'

* * *

'I should describe a great deal of modern music as "laboratory" music or better still as not music at all. Many modern composers have gone down the wrong path. They are no longer making music, but contortions and gestures in sound. They are trying to do something unnatural – like walking with their feet in the air.'

* * *

In the 1950s, Casals gave a series of interviews with J. Ma. Corredor, the Catalan writer and activist, for *Conversations with Casals*, in which he attacked 'modern' music mercilessly:

Corredor: Furtwängler says that contemporary

music 'has a limited number of listeners but nevertheless these are passionately convinced ones'.

Casals: It must be an artificial passion since there is so often nothing to understand in this music. These 'passionate' people form a minority – and they don't understand either.

Corredor challenged Casals further.

Corredor: Some works now regarded as masterpieces have taken a long time to become recognised.

Casals: If familiarity is necessary for comprehension, then the chaotic music of which I speak has had more than enough time to establish itself. The reason why the public does not want to hear this music is not because it is new. What they feel is that it lacks human warmth.

Next, they discussed the increased use of atonality.

Corredor: Atonal music, people say, is a reflection of the uncertainty of the chaotic period in which we live.

Casals: Music should be used as a means of keeping alive an ideal, not for the propaganda of morbid and destructive tendencies. Why should an artist be obsessed by the uncertainties of our time? Instead he should react against them by showing his faith in those human values which have survived so many catastrophes. Music cannot be the slave of these uncertainties. However dark our times may seem, music should bring a message of hope.

Casals was also sceptical of modern opera.

Corredor: Did you know Alban Berg?
Casals: No.
Corredor: Have you seen *Wozzeck*?
Casals: I only heard a recording of it on the radio.
Corredor: What impression did this work make on you?
Casals: That of a master who moves in a world that is not mine.

* * *

Certain contemporary composers responded none-too-kindly to Casals's obstinate dismissal of their art. After watching a television programme about Casals, Igor Stravinsky – widely considered one of the most influential composers of the twentieth century – remarked:

That was an interesting programme. In one scene the cellist and a sort of Hungarian composer, Zoltán Kodály, are seen together with their great-granddaughters, at least that's what one supposes until one learns that they are their wives. And what were the two racy octogenarians talking about? Well, they were saying that the trouble with *me* is that I must always be doing the latest thing. But who are they to talk, when they have been doing the same old thing for at least eighty years! Señor Casals also offered us an interesting insight into his philosophy – for example, playing Bach in the style of Brahms.

On pop music

'What, maestro, is your opinion of rock 'n' roll?'
'Poison put to sound – a brutalisation of both life and art.'

* * *

'Señor Casals, allow me to introduce you to our new singing star,' said the hotel manager.

'Lovely, lovely, how nice! What are you singing? Lieder, Brahms, Schubert…?'

'No, no! He is the great pop star. His records make *millions*.'

'Oh,' replied Casals.

On Picasso

'Do not tell me that anyone can understand Picasso when he paints a woman with five noses protruding from different parts of her body. How can anyone get anything out of such nonsense? It is inhuman!'

On music

'They call me a great cellist. I am not a cellist; I am a musician. That is much more important.'

* * *

'The first musical commandment is total respect for the music.'

* * *

'Complete understanding of a work of music does not come altogether intuitively or at once. One must perceive the structure of the music, understand the different elements and the relationships between the notes.

'The true artist must seek the meaning of the music and this will only be found if he sets about his work honestly, persistently and with humility.'

* * *

'As in any other artistic activity, music has no definite boundaries.'

* * *

'Music is like speech. If necessary, you even have to make sure to accentuate every syllable. The expression of music consists of giving each note its own value with due regard to what is going to follow – exactly as we should do when we talk.'

* * *

'What purpose can music – or any form of art – serve if it does not speak in a language everyone can understand?'

* * *

'Music – that wonderful universal language – should be a source of communication among men. Again I implore my fellow musicians throughout the world to put the purity of their art at the service of mankind in order to unite all races. Let each of us contribute as much as he can until this ideal is attained in all its glory.'

On war and peace

'When the Cold War had become intense and the fear of atomic war spread throughout the world, I embarked on a peace crusade of my own with the only weapon I have at my command – my music. I had written an oratorio based on the Nativity called *El Pessebre* ("The Manger") and I began taking this oratorio to the capitals of many lands.'

* * *

'I always instinctively hated violence.'

* * *

'Throughout the atrocious years of the First World

War, I was tormented by the very question that I had put to myself as a young man in Barcelona, when I first discovered the misery of the world. The question was: was man created in order to suffer as terribly as this? The life of a single child is worth more to me than the whole of music, and yet it was thanks to music that I was able to preserve my mental health in the midst of the world's insanity. For me, music continued to be an affirmation of the beauty capable of being created by man: the same man who was now perpetrating so many crimes and unleashing so much suffering.'

* * *

'I think that if all the mothers of the world would tell their sons, "You were not born to kill or to be killed, so do not fight," there would be no more war.'

* * *

On the night of the Spanish Revolution, Casals was rehearsing L'Orquestra Pau Casals at the Orfeó Català in Barcelona. They were to perform Beethoven's Ninth Symphony the next day at the same Montjuïc auditorium where the orchestra had helped celebrate the birth of the Republic only five years before.

Casals had rehearsed the first three movements and the chorus had come on to the platform ready to begin the final 'Ode to Joy' when a messenger handed him a note from the Minister of Culture, Ventura Gassol: a military revolt was due any minute and the rehearsal should cease immediately so that the musicians would have time to return to their homes. Casals read the note aloud to the orchestra and asked whether they would like to leave at once or say farewell by completing the symphony.

They played to the end.

Casals's eyes were filled with tears as the chorus sang the immortal words in Catalan: 'All mankind are brothers.' 'One day,' he promised, 'we will perform the Ninth Symphony when peace is with us again.'

The orchestra and the chorus returned to their homes through streets already thick with barricades.

*   *   *

'We live in an age in which we have accomplished magnificent things and made miraculous advances, an age in which man embarks upon the exploration of the stars. Yet on our planet we continue to act like barbarians. Like barbarians, we fear our neighbours on the earth; we arm against them and they arm against us. The time has come when this must be halted if man is to survive. We must become accustomed to the fact that we are human beings.'

On politics

Casals's views on politics were every bit as forceful as his views on music. When asked why (having chosen to live in exile) he refused to give up his Spanish passport, he snapped: 'Spain is my country. Let Franco give up his.'

* * *

Refusing an invitation to meet Sir Stafford Cripps (then the British Chancellor of the Exchequer), Casals reasoned: 'We would not understand one another. He would be speaking about politics and I about morality.'

* * *

'An affront to human dignity is an affront to me, and to protest against injustice is a matter of conscience. Are human rights of less importance to an artist than to other men? Does being an artist exempt him from his obligations as a man? If anything, the artist has an even greater responsibility, because he has been granted special sensitivities and perceptions and because his voice may be heard when others may not. Who, indeed, should be more concerned than the artist about the defence of liberty and free inquiry? Such fundamentals are essential to his very creativity.'

* * *

'To see people gathered together in a concert hall came to have a symbolic significance for me. When I looked into their faces, and we shared the beauty of music, I knew that we were brothers and sisters, all members of the same family. Despite the dreadful conflicts of the intervening years and all the false barriers between nations, that knowledge has never left me. It will remain with me until the end. I long for the day when the peoples of the world will sit together, bound by happiness and love of beauty, as in one great concert hall!'

*   *   *

On 19 October 1938, as Franco's army advanced steadily nearer to Catalonia, Casals was rehearsing for what proved to be his last concert in Spain. The orchestra contained many former members of L'Orquestra Pau Casals and, after playing overtures by Gluck and Weber under Casals's direction, they accompanied him in the Haydn and Dvořák concertos. During the rehearsal there was an air raid and the orchestra quickly dispersed to the auditorium. Casals, however, remained on the platform, picked up a cello and began to play a Bach suite. Gradually the orchestra returned to their places and the rehearsal continued.

The concert was broadcast internationally and, during the interval, Casals spoke movingly over the radio, warning that Spain's freedom was in grave danger and repeating the message in English and French.

In free Spain, work was halted for two hours on

a Wednesday afternoon to allow people to hear the broadcast.

* * *

Support for Casals's humanitarian stance came from all over the world. At a concert at the Royal Albert Hall in June 1945, a crowd of at least 10,000 people thronged the hall. The crush was so great that police had to clear the way for his car while the crowd chanted: '*Viva Casals, Viva Casals.*' The German writer Emil Ludwig compared Casals's reception from the people of London to that accorded to Winston Churchill. Casals said afterwards: 'I could sense very distinctly admiration for the artist, affection for me as a person and, above all, support of my attitude.'

* * *

In an interview given shortly after the end of the Second World War, Casals said:

History will always preserve the memory of how the British people kept the flame of civilization alive in wartime, and I am glad that I have lived to see such things are possible. I was old enough when this war started and I am older still today, but let me say that I have lived fully during these years. I have survived all these great changes throughout the world. I have seen the collapse of the two most hateful forms of dictatorship, and living through them has given me renewed strength.

*   *   *

A journalist from Barcelona asked Casals his opinion on the Spanish Revolution:

If the Revolution is justice and equality, if it is not a simple changing of coats, if it is not a conflict of egotisms and the satisfaction of hates and personal scores and if it will flower tomorrow in human happiness, I accept and identify myself with it. I am an artist and with my art seek only peace and harmony among men.

*   *   *

'Any form of government is acceptable to me, provided it has been chosen by the people.'

*   *   *

'The very idea of hating Jews is incomprehensible to me. My own life has been so enriched by tender associations with Jewish fellow artists and friends. Of course they make wonderful musicians. The reason is that they have so much heart – yes, and head, too! When I am conducting and tell the orchestra members, "Play Jewish," they know what I mean.*

'My friend Sasha Schneider sometimes says to me, "You know, Don Pablo, you are really Jewish." He will not listen to my claim that my parents were Catholic and I am a Catalan. He shakes his head good-naturedly and says, "No, you are wrong. You may have been born of Catholic parents in Catalonia, but actually you are Jewish. For you could not play as you do

---

*   Casals's choice of language reflects the sensibilities of his time.

if you were not." I tell Sasha that there are exceptions to his rule.'

* * *

'Casals believed in the necessity of giving a good kick to those who dare to trespass upon other people's rights. Once, when we were walking on the beach together, he said: "Am I free to walk on your feet? … Freedom must not be abused."' – Paul Tortelier

* * *

'I have always been opposed to extreme nationalism. The people of one nation are not superior to the people of any other – different, yes, but superior, no. Extreme nationalists believe they have the right to dominate other nations. Patriotism is something wholly different. Love of one's soil is deep in the nature of man.'

* * *

'Casals was a surprising man. One morning the

papers carried a front-page story about the assassi-
nation of a Spanish Minister of State by the Catalan
anarchist Ferrer, who had shot him point-blank while
parliament was in session. When I spoke of it with
indignation to the great cellist, he said impassively:
"Ferrer has simply done his duty. I am myself an anarchist."' – Artur Rubinstein

*　*　*

'Casals respected Furtwängler not only as a man of
integrity but as a fine musician. So I asked Casals if
he would like to record Brahms's Double Concerto
with me, with Furtwängler as conductor. "Yes, certainly," he said, but the correspondence dragged on
for two or three years. Whenever I tried to finalise a
date, there was always an obstacle. Finally, I received
a letter which, with disarming frankness, betrayed
the limits of his independence: "You will recall that I
told you nothing would give me more pleasure than
to record with Furtwängler. I still feel he is a man
of integrity. However, I am seen by my colleagues in
New York as a symbol of anti-fascism, and I would

let them down if I played under Furtwängler. They wouldn't understand." In other words, he was prepared to let me know that he didn't have the courage of his convictions; so long as those convictions were approved by his admirers, they were strong convictions indeed, but in other circumstances not strong enough to withstand guilt by association with a man wrongfully accused. It was an honest letter and a disappointing one.' – Yehudi Menuhin, violinist and conductor

As a man

During a conversation with Casals on the role of the artist as a public figure, Albert Schweitzer observed: 'It is better to create than to protest.'

'Why not do both?' asked Casals. 'Why not create *and* protest – do both?'

*   *   *

Announcing his intention to embark on a crusade for world peace, Casals declared:

I am a man first, an artist second. As a man, my first obligation is to the welfare of my fellow men. I will endeavour to meet this obligation through music

– the means which God has given me – since it tran-
scends language, politics and national boundaries.
My contribution to world peace may be small, but
at least I will have given all I can to an ideal I hold
sacred.

*   *   *

'I have never felt that music, or any other art form,
can be an answer in itself. A musician is also a man
and his attitude to life is more important than his
music. The two *cannot* be separated.'

*   *   *

'His art, for all its impetuousness, is allied to a rigid
refusal to compromise with wrong, with anything that
is morally squalid or offensive to justice – and this, in
a way, ennobles and broadens our understanding of
the artist, setting an example, in our corrupt times,
of proud incorruptible integrity.' – Thomas Mann,
novelist and Nobel Laureate for literature in 1929

* * *

'I know that there are those who believe that an artist should live in an ivory tower, apart from his fellow men. That is a concept to which I have never been able to subscribe.'

* * *

'The greatest human experience is the love of all humanity, the love that goes out to the entire world… more important than the love of a man for a woman. To know that is to know the meaning of life. For then you understand suffering. Everything is more important than music when it is a question of human pain. Everything that is human is more important than one's feeling of love for something beautiful, for music, for paintings. How can there be any doubt? Humanity is far more important than music. You can do much for humanity with music, with anything noble. But greater than all is love – love for all that lives.'

* * *

'I believe the capacity to *care* is the thing which gives life its deepest significance and meaning.'

* * *

'There are people who do not love animals, but I think this is because they do not understand them. For me, animals have always been a special part of the wonder of nature – the smallest as well as the largest – with their amazing variety and fascinating habits. I am captivated by their spirit. And I find in them a longing to communicate and a real capacity for love. If, sometimes, they do not trust but fear man, it is because man has treated them with such arrogance and insensitivity.'

* * *

'I am an artist, but in the practice of my art I am, after all, just a manual worker – and have been all my life.'

* * *

In a letter to Albert E. Kahn, author of *Joys and Sorrows*,* Casals explained – characteristically – why he consistently declined to write an autobiography: 'I do not happen to feel my life deserves commemoration in an autobiography. I have only done what I had to do.'

* * *

'What was it that was so compelling about "this unobtrusive little man?"' asked one admirer. 'Physically unimpressive, he would steal quietly into the room – yet radiate an unaccountable sense of power and authority. It was the same sensation you sometimes get in an art gallery when a certain painting suddenly claims all your attention and you feel yourself becoming more and more drawn to it.'

* * *

---

* Casals's series of autobiographical interviews.

A pupil recalled: 'It was impossible to sit in the same room with Casals and emerge unchanged.'

* * *

When Casals learned that the Royal Philharmonic Society was experiencing financial difficulties after playing at one of their concerts in December 1926, he immediately returned the fee of 100 guineas he had received with a letter intimating that if a well-worded appeal was sent to him he would sign its and get other famous artists to endorse it.

'I could never have believed', he said during his speech at a dinner after the concert,

that a musical institution of such unique tradition and standing would have to endure such a struggle – only to find itself on the verge of extinction. Both private and official interest must be aroused in this country to avoid it being dissolved. Gentlemen! The Philharmonic Society must not go out of existence! All the world knows what it represents.

* * *

'The core of any important human enterprise or activity must be character and kindness.'

* * *

In one of John Barbirolli's first London concerts, Casals was the soloist in Haydn's D major Concerto. During the rehearsal the orchestra became increasingly restless with Barbirolli's detailed approach to their opening *tutti*. As the murmuring increased, Casals interrupted: 'Gentlemen, listen to him – he *knows*.'

Barbirolli never forgot that moment, later recalling: 'Only a great man would have uttered those words for a very young boy.'

* * *

At the height of the Blitz, Casals was advised not to play in London under any circumstances as the capital was under heavy bombardment every day.

'Nothing would please me more,' retorted Casals. 'What I most enjoy is standing up for something.'

* * *

Casals would not allow either himself or a fellow artist to be taken advantage of and would certainly make a stand if he felt the occasion demanded.

At a rehearsal in Brussels, he found the hall already crowded with an audience who had apparently paid to gain admission. Casals immediately refused to play on the grounds that he was only being paid for the concert, *not* for the rehearsal. Finally, the concert manager relented: 'Maestro, I am obliged to *beg* you to play – the audience are expecting it. I will pay you an additional concert fee, and you may consider your-self engaged for two performances.'

Casals had therefore established a precedent for all artists to collect a rehearsal fee – but not before explaining to the orchestra's director that he had only acted to protest against a rule he felt to be unjust.

'Now,' he declared, 'I will only keep the fee we

originally agreed. Here is the second one – it must be given to the orchestra.'

*   *   *

'It is not so important to be considered nice; it is more important to play well.'

*   *   *

When a young lady cellist was arrested (and fined) for giving a recital in a topless dress, the judge remarked: 'I don't think Casals would play the cello better without his pants.'

Questioned on this, Casals commented: 'I'm not sure, I've never played with them off.'

*   *   *

Casals's response to certain events would often startle his friends and colleagues. Watching the television transmission of man's first steps on the moon, he declared: 'It will soon be forgotten.'

This provoked much heated disagreement, until one friend suddenly realised that Casals had, over the course of his life, watched transportation develop from horseback to interplanetary travel.

* * *

'The moment we stop experimenting, we stop altogether.'

* * *

'Sometimes I look about me with a feeling of complete dismay. In the confusion that afflicts the world today, I see a disrespect for the very values of life. Beauty is all around us, but how many are blind to it! Man looks at the wonders of this earth and yet seems to see nothing. People live hectically but give little thought to where they are going. They seek excitement merely for its own sake, as if they were lost and desperate.'

* * *

'Just as there is in man an infinite capacity for good, there is also an infinite capacity for evil. I have long recognised within myself the potential for great evil – of the worst crime – just as I have within me the potential for great good. Every one of us has within himself the possibilities for both.'

On religion

'I see divine origin everywhere: in music, the sea, a flower, a leaf, an act of kindness. In all those things I see the presence of what people call God. And I have this divine strain in myself; that is what tells me of the existence of that higher something, so high that I am obliged to believe in it. And I see divinity in the miracle of music more than in anything else. The sounds created by a Bach or a Mozart are a miracle that nobody can explain without thinking of something infinitely good – something divine.'

* * *

'I cannot believe that these marvels which surround us – the miracle which is life – can come from nothing. How can something come from nothing? The miracle must come from somewhere. It comes from God.'

On genius

'The only credit we can claim is for the use we make of the talent we have been given. That is why I tell young musicians, "Do not be vain because you happen to have talent. *You* are not responsible for that – it was not of your making. It is what you make of your talent that matters. You must cherish this gift. Do not waste what you have been given – work, work constantly and nourish it."'

* * *

'For the artist of genius, the hour of recognition always arrives.'

* * *

'All great artists are innovators.'

* * *

'Genius escapes all definition. How can one define sublimity – or even the charm of a flower?'

* * *

'Genius forms itself, and professors – however eminent – contribute only to a very modest extent to its development.'

As a teacher

'I can think of no profession more important than teaching. A good teacher, a *real* teacher, can be like a second father to his pupil.'

* * *

'To teach is to learn.'

* * *

'I will say nothing complicated, only elemental things – as everything ought to be – beginning with life. But you must know that the simplest things are the ones that count.'

* * *

During a masterclass on Bach's Fifth Suite, Casals struck the octave C, which begins the work, with such force that his student jumped visibly. With a gleam in his eye Casals looked up and asked: '*Pourquoi pas?*'

* * *

'Break your cello! It is better to have character than have a beautiful sound.'

* * *

When the cellist Bernard Greenhouse arrived at Casals's house for an audition at ten o'clock one morning, he was a little surprised to be greeted by an unshaven maestro still wearing his pyjamas. Casals told Greenhouse to begin warming up while he finished his *toilette*. Greenhouse played away happily to himself, but after half an hour or so he became increasingly puzzled: where on earth was Casals? That moment, his eye caught sight of a slight movement in the mirror – Casals's bald head was retreating rapidly behind the door.

'I wanted to hear you play when you weren't nervous,' said an embarrassed Casals, after admitting he'd been listening all the time.

His 'audition' over, Greenhouse began lessons with a Bach suite, but it seemed that Casals expected nothing less than an exact replica of his own playing, down to the last details of fingering and bowing, and the tiniest subtleties of interpretation. Greenhouse grew increasingly rebellious, as he felt that he was simply being forced to produce a mirror image of Casals's performance.

At one lesson, Greenhouse was on the point of protesting when Casals took his cello and told him to listen carefully. Greenhouse watched in awe as Casals recreated the same piece of music. *Everything* was different – bowings, fingerings and interpretation – yet it was just as beautiful. Greenhouse felt freed. Casals had forced him to assimilate the style and structure of the work until it had become second nature and had then shown the aspiring cellist there is no definitive interpretation: that every time a work is played there are limitless possibilities for its recreation.

*   *   *

As a pupil was about to make his first, tentative entry in Dvořák's Concerto, Casals leapt up and cried: 'Announce the hero!'

*   *   *

Like many of the greatest teachers, Casals was most concerned with developing each pupil's finer qualities rather than constantly harping on their faults. Gregor Piatigorsky, who went on to have an international solo career lasting more than forty years, thought his first meeting with Casals gave an interesting insight into his approach as a teacher:

I was introduced to Pablo Casals, a little bald man with a pipe. He said he was pleased to meet young musicians such as Rudolf Serkin and me. Serkin, who stood stiffly next to me seemed, like myself, to be fighting his diffidence. Rudi had played before my arrival, and Casals now wanted to hear us together. Beethoven's D major Sonata was on the piano.

'Why don't you play it?' asked Casals. Both nervous and barely knowing each other, we gave a poor performance that terminated somewhere in the middle.

'Bravo! Bravo! Wonderful!' Casals applauded. Next, Casals wanted to hear the Schumann Concerto. I never played worse. Casals asked for Bach. Exasperated, I obliged with a performance matching the Beethoven and Schumann.

'Splendid! *Magnifique!*' said Casals, embracing me.

Bewildered, I left the house. I knew how badly I had played, but why did he, the master, have to praise and embrace me? This apparent insincerity pained me more than anything else. The greater was my shame and delight when, a few years later, I met Casals in Paris. We had dinner together and played duets for two cellos, and I played for him until late at night. Spurred by his great warmth, and happy, I confessed what I had thought of his praising me in Berlin. He reacted with sudden anger. He rushed to the cello.

'Listen!' He played a phrase from the Beethoven Sonata. 'Didn't you use this fingering? Ah, you did! It was novel to me… it was good… and here, didn't you attack that passage with an up-bow, like this?' He demonstrated. He went through Schumann and Bach, always emphasising all he liked that I had done.

'And for the rest,' he said, with a gesture of dismissal, 'leave it to the ignorant and stupid who judge by counting only the faults. I can be grateful, and so must you be, for just one note, one wonderful phrase.'

I left with the feeling of having been with a great artist and a friend.

* * *

Of an English cellist with rather fat fingers who went to study with Casals it was said that 'he left with sausages and came home with bangers'.

* * *

Casals began working with a beginner, and after many arduous lessons the boy made rapid progress but, Casals realised, without any sense of direction. Everything he played seemed to be ridden with gimmicks rather than based on true foundations. Casals was disturbed but nevertheless pleased enough with the boy's progress to consent to him giving his first public performance.

Casals set out for the concert with great expectations, but he was soon dismayed by what he considered to be a display of appalling vulgarity. 'What kind of teacher can you be?' thought Casals to himself. 'That young fool played with all his old arrogant self-confidence. Rhythm, discretion, control, were thrown to the winds, and what came forth was an impudent array of vulgarity. Not one cheap effect did he miss. It was a caricature of the music – and worse than a caricature!'

Casals decided not to go backstage, thinking it would be better to try and analyse the catastrophe at the next day's lesson. By then he was almost eager to hear his pupil offer the excuse of extreme nervousness, but it was not to be.

'*Maître*!' exclaimed the boy, 'this was my first public appearance. I realised I had to forget everything you'd taught me, otherwise people would think I was another Casals! I had to let my own personality speak.'

'Get out of here,' shouted Casals,

and never let me see your face again! Personality! I have not taught you anything of my personality, nor could I. It would be easier to graft my fingers on to yours... What I have tried to teach you, imbecile that you are, is a true, simple and reverent regard for music. But you haven't the character to see it. The shabby costume you falsely call 'personality' will neither cover nor disguise the vacuum that lies beneath.

* * *

'An artist has complete responsibility for the music he plays.'

* * *

'For me, organisation is essential to creative work, and I often give my pupils this motto: "Freedom... and order."'

* * *

'Intonation is a matter of conscience. You know when a note is wrong in the same way you know when you do something wrong in life. We must not continue to do the wrong thing.'

On technique

'I have always regarded technique as a means, not as an end in itself. One must, of course, master technique, but, at the same time, one must not become enslaved by it. The true purpose of technique is to transmit the inner meaning, the message, of the music.'

*　　*　　*

'The most perfect technique is that which is not noticed at all.'

*　　*　　*

'I started to make certain changes to the accepted

techniques of cello playing when I was at school in Barcelona. It is true I was only twelve or so at the time, but certain things are obvious, even to children. And it was obvious to me that there was something very awkward and unnatural in playing with a stiff arm, with one's elbows close to one's sides, as cellists were taught in those days. As a matter of fact, we were even told to hold a book under the armpit of our bowing arm while we were learning! That all seemed foolish to me. So I began to devise a method of playing which would free the arms and get rid of that very cramped and artificial position... Today nobody learns the cello with a book under his armpit!'

Pablo Casals at the time of his
Parisian debut, aged twenty-two.
© Royal College of Music

A tribute from one of Casals's admirers
after his outstanding performances
in Brazil, part of his tour of South
America in 1904. © Fundación Pau Casals

A studio photograph of Casals, taken in
New York, with the two items he could
not do without: his pipe and his cello.
© Royal College of Music

Casals playing mini golf.
© Atelier Peter Moeschlin SWB

Another day, another
masterclass. Even at
the tender age of twelve,
Casals rejected the
'cramped and artificial
position' he was taught
and forged his own
technique of playing
with 'free arms'.
© Atelier Peter Moeschlin SWB

One of the most enduring images of Casals was as 'a little bald man with a pipe'. In Casals's own words: 'I smoke as much as I can.' © Atelier Peter Moeschlin SWB

Casals with Albert Schweitzer, a theologian and Nobel Peace Prize winner. The two bonded over their love of Bach, and in 1958, they called for an end to the arms race and nuclear testing. © Atelier Peter Moeschlin SWB

'Crowned with laurels', a sketch made of Casals before he received an honorary doctorate from the University of Edinburgh, alongside Albert Schweitzer, in 1934. © Fundación Pau Casals

Casals at the White House in 1961, where he played for President John F. Kennedy. It was Casals's first concert on US soil since he ceased performing in 1946 to protest against the Allies' decision to leave General Franco's regime unchallenged after the war (although in 1958 he had played at the neutral ground of the United Nations headquarters in New York).
© John F. Kennedy Library

A sketch of Casals with his ever-present pipe.
© Fundación Pau Casals

On intuition and interpretation

'I have always believed that intuition is the decisive element in both the composing and performance of music.'

* * *

'The written note is like a straitjacket, whereas music – like life itself – is constant movement, constant spontaneity, free from all restrictions.'

* * *

'The art of interpretation is *not* to play what is written.'

* * *

'I have heard so many violinists and cellists, and they are all wonderful. Yet afterwards one thinks, "How curious, he plays so well, but… I feel monotony, lack of colour, a lack of variation in the playing."'

* * *

'It is better to do something in bad taste than to be monotonous.'

* * *

'The heart of a melody can never be put down on paper.'

* * *

Once, when rehearsing Dvořák's Concerto, the conductor leaned over and asked Casals what speed he would like for the next movement.

'The right one,' came the terse reply.

* * *

'How can we expect to create a vital performance if we don't rethink a work every time? Each spring the leaves on the trees reappear, but each spring they are different.'

*   *   *

'What really matters is the result, not the method.'

On recording

During his 1945 recording of Elgar's Concerto with Sir Adrian Boult, Casals's legendary grunting could be heard so clearly over the microphones that the distraught recording engineer could contain himself no longer.

'Maestro,' he protested, 'I'm afraid we're picking up all your grunts.'

'In that case,' replied Casals, singularly unmoved, 'you can charge double for the record.'

*　*　*

'Casals was recording the Haydn D major Concerto. At one very difficult passage he was not satisfied with his playing and asked for a repeat. The next take there was a distinct "fluff" in his playing at the same place. He stopped and the section was started yet again. This time an overwrought string player made a "domino". Once again we began the section and approached the passage with obvious tension: Casals tripped even more noticeably. It was an unheard-of occurrence, for Casals was considered above any such faulty playing. The atmosphere was electric, with everyone thoroughly on edge. Casals stood up, turned to the conductor and orchestra, and with a slight smile said: "Gentlemen, I am sorry, but today I can play no more. Tomorrow, with your help, gentlemen, *tomorrow* we make well."

'Tomorrow we did indeed "make well". Casals appeared, smiling and relaxed, and played the tiresome passage over and over again perfectly – smiling at the orchestra – before we began the recording. His confidence was communicated to everybody and the recording proceeded without further hitch.' – Archie Camden, principal bassoonist with the BBC Symphony Orchestra

* * *

At a masterclass on Boccherini's Concerto, Casals began to demonstrate the opening, only to be interrupted by his pupil: 'But maestro! That's not how you play it on your recording.'

'That may be so,' Casals snapped. 'But *this* time is the right way to play it!'

On agents and impresarios

At twenty-seven, when Casals gave the 1904 New York premiere of Strauss's *Don Quixote* with the great composer himself conducting, he had already begun to go bald.

'If only you would wear a wig,' lamented his New York manager. 'Then I could get much higher fees for your appearances.'

When Casals – inevitably – refused, the enterprising manager put out a story that the young cellist's premature baldness was entirely caused by the fact that he had given a lock of hair to every woman he had loved!

* * *

Interviewer: I understand that at Ysaÿe's home in Belgium you used to play piano quintets with Kreisler, Thibaud and Ysaÿe on the strings and Cortot or Busoni on the piano. Combinations like that would have made the impresarios go crazy!

Casals: That's why impresarios were not admitted to these meetings.

* * *

Halfway through an American tour, Casals discovered that his New York agent was charging the promoters considerably more than he'd been led to believe and was simply pocketing the difference. This amounted to several hundred dollars a concert which, in those days, was a great deal of money. Rather than say anything immediately, he continued to watch over the situation until, when the tour was over, he invited his manager to meet him at his hotel with the promise that the conversation would not take up much time. The meeting arranged, Casals began his plan of campaign. Placing two chairs near the hotel entrance, he ushered the man to the seat nearest the door. After a few pleasantries the agent enquired how everything had gone. 'Just fine,' replied Casals, 'apart from the fact that you've been robbing me.' Immediately the man rose, pale and flustered, and Casals leapt into action. Shoving him into the hotel's revolving doors, he began to spin them round and round as fast as he could until, suddenly, they broke. For a few seconds, Casals watched his former agent hobbling off down the street before the hotel manager called him back to pay for the damage.

On America

'At last I felt I was in a society where merit – whatever inequities had yet to be solved – was judged by character and capability. For me, at the age of twenty-four, America was an emancipation.' – Casals reminiscing on his first American tour

* * *

'Never before had I been so overwhelmed by Nature's grandeur and diversity; and never before had I been more conscious of the invincible spirit of man – man who had penetrated these spaces and made them his home. You felt mankind could have accomplished anything and that all things were possible here.

'The New World ceased to be a mere phrase to me. Newness abounded on all sides. One sensed a nation still in the process of its creation – like a great symphony in rehearsal.'

* * *

Casals's first tour of America was in 1901, during which he gave concerts with the pianist Léon Moreau and enjoyed several unusual adventures along the way. Displaying a characteristic interest in his fellow men, he determined, one afternoon, to find out what life was like down a coalmine:

It was fascinating down there in the mine. Moreau and I became so engrossed that we completely lost track of the time and forgot all about the concert that evening. When we remembered, we had to rush straight from the coalmine to the concert hall. We had no time to change or even wash our faces. You can imagine the looks we got from the audience as we took the stage covered in soot from head to toe!

Another episode found Moreau and Casals in a small town which resembled the set of a Western movie:

One day Moreau and I were out for a stroll and wandered into the saloon. We were soon involved in a poker game with several cowboys – surly-looking fellows with guns in their belts. My experience of gambling was limited, but I was lucky enough – or perhaps I should say unlucky enough – to start winning consistently. As the silver coins began to pile up, I noticed the faces of the other card players growing increasingly grim and a tense mood settled over the game. I looked uneasily at their revolvers and began to wonder whether our concert tour might come to a very abrupt and unforeseen conclusion! By this time everyone was drinking and one of the cowboys offered me a glass of whisky. I refused as politely as I could, saying that I didn't drink while gambling. The cowboy snarled: '*Here* we drink *and* gamble!' I drank.

Finally the cards began to change and I was fortunate enough to start losing – to the visible approval of my companions. Suddenly everyone was smiling, and when Moreau and I finally rose to leave, we all hugged one another and parted like old friends.

* * *

'When I went to Washington to play for President Kennedy [in 1961], some newspapers reported that this was my first appearance at the White House. Actually, I had played there previously for President Roosevelt – not Franklin D. Roosevelt but *Theodore* Roosevelt. That was during my visit to America in 1904.

'The performance took place at a reception given by President Kennedy. He had an infectious joviality. After the concert he put his arm around my shoulders and led me among the guests, introducing me to everyone and talking all the time. In a sense I felt that he personified the American nation, with all his energy, strength and confidence. It wasn't hard to picture him galloping on a horse or hunting big game, as I'm told he was so fond of doing.'

On communism

Casals often recalled the sense of suffocation he felt during his first trip to Russia in 1905:

> When you go through Customs, you meet these enormous officials who treat you with suspicion and immediately you feel as if you are entering a prison.
>
> When the cataclysm broke in 1917, I was not surprised. Yet the way in which some people I knew were treated made me loathe the new regime just as intensely as the old.

He was particularly shocked by an incident that took place after a recital at the palace of a Russian prince. As he was leaving, he was surprised to encounter a corridor lined with servants, and grew even more astonished when they threw themselves to the floor before him. Casals looked at the prince enquiringly.

'Walk over them,' said the Russian. 'That's what they're there for.'

*　*　*

'During the spiritual crisis I went through when I was fifteen, I even turned to the works of Karl Marx in the hope of finding some solution to the problem of life – but I didn't. The idea of the brotherhood of man is wonderful, but it has been perverted by communism. Without liberty, man cannot follow his destiny – and communism is the negation of liberty.'

On England

In August 1899, Casals and Ernest Walker, a young English pianist, travelled by train to Southampton and then took the ferry to the Isle of Wight, where they were to play before Her Majesty Queen Victoria at the royal residence, Osborne House. Before the performance they were introduced to Her Majesty who, then nearly eighty, had ruled the British Empire since 1837. Casals and Walker settled on stage to play Fauré's Elegy. After they had finished, the Queen – much against custom – moved over to the duo and addressed them. After congratulating Casals, she said that Queen María Cristina of Spain had spoken highly of him, and she hoped his career would soon repay the honour and trust invested in it.

Later that night, before retiring, she made the following entry in her diary:

Osborne. August 2nd 1899. – After dinner a young Spaniard, Señor Casals, played on the violoncello most beautifully. He is a very modest young man whom the Queen of Spain has had educated, and from whom he received his fine instrument. He has a splendid tone and plays with much execution and feeling.

On tour

Casals first encountered the problem of travelling with a cello when he was detained and interrogated at great length by security police at the Dutch border. His identity papers failed to satisfy them, likewise his explanation that he had come to Holland to play for Queen Wilhelmina's coronation celebrations in 1890. Eventually, after many hours – during which his cello and case were scrupulously examined – he was allowed on his way.

Fourteen years later, at a dinner at the home of Professor de Lange, director of the Amsterdam Conservatoire, the professor was abruptly summoned from the table only to return, minutes later, his face reddened with laughter. Apparently, the police had called at the door enquiring about his 'suspicious' guest. It seemed Casals bore an uncanny resemblance to a dangerous anarchist and had consequently been under constant surveillance whenever he set foot on Dutch soil. Professor de Lange calmed the official by explaining that Casals was only a dangerous anarchist in matters of Bach interpretation.

* * *

One night in Rio, Casals and Harold Bauer found themselves with nowhere to stay, as a business convention had booked every hotel in the city. After tramping the streets for several hours, they finally stumbled across a shabby little boarding house near the waterfront; there was only a single room, but it would be better than nothing.

Soon after they had fallen, exhausted, into bed, Casals was awoken by a repeated metallic clicking sound. In this place, he thought, it could be anything. Calling to Bauer, he tugged at the light switch and immediately revealed the cause of the disturbance: the place was infested with cockroaches. Hundreds had appeared all over the walls, and a couple had even started work on Bauer's toenails. The two men began an immediate extermination campaign with the soles of their shoes, and quickly learned what revolting aromas the unsightly creatures emit when smashed.

The next day, they changed hotel.

*　　*　　*

Following a concert in Rio, a lengthy dinner party was held and it was nearly dawn by the time Casals and Bauer returned to their hotel, complete with their concert takings – a large sum of extremely dirty bank notes which they had stuffed in a suitcase. As no one could be found so late to take care of the money, both men decided it should be safe enough in their room for what little remained of the night.

They awoke to find the door wide open and the room in complete disarray. Casals's cello had been removed from its case but lay undamaged on the floor and, incredibly, even the suitcase stuffed with bank notes remained untouched. But everything else had gone: watches, passports – even the studs and cufflinks from their shirts. The hotel manager and the police were summoned, and eventually two suspects were detained – one a dapper-looking gentleman who had been caught with Casals's visiting card in his pocket.

Casals and Bauer debated the incident for the rest of the day. How on earth could the thieves have broken in without either of them hearing a thing? Casals held the theory that the burglars must have used some kind of chemical gas to render them senseless, although Bauer pointed out – more realistically – that they had both consumed considerable quantities of the local wine at dinner.

Years later, an indignant Casals read in a newspaper that the police had captured the infamous and elusive robber known as 'The King of the Pickpockets'. Alongside the article was a photo of that same dapper gentleman the police had detained in Rio.

'You see!' said Casals proudly. 'I wasn't robbed by some petty amateur but by the profession's top artist!'

On Spain

'I have been to many countries in the course of my life and have come across many beautiful places. But the beauty that I remember as being the most pure is the beauty of Catalonia. If I close my eyes, I can evoke the sea along the coast at San Salvador, or the little town of Sitges with its fishing boats pulled up on the beach; I can see the cattle, vineyards and olive groves of the province of Tarragona, the banks of the River Llobregat or the high peaks of Montserrat. Catalonia is the land of my birth, and I love her like a mother...'

* * *

'I have never cared for bullfighting; it revolts me.'

Married to Marta

'I have observed a curious trait in many men – though they do not hesitate to say how much they love their mothers, they are seldom heard to say how much they love their wives!'

* * *

'Marta is the great love in my whole life, the only true love. She fills everything in me and has made up for all the emptiness in my life. Nothing can be compared to our perfect love and our ideal life together. It is a feeling I have never experienced before. I had never been happy, and I only found real happiness with Marta.'

* * *

'Recently I couldn't manage to open a carton of cottage cheese. Exasperated, I called out to my wife, "Marta, I can't do anything with my hands!"

'"That's not entirely true, Pablo," she said, pointing at my cello standing in the corner.'

On age

'Age is the glory of the great, don't you think?' wrote Casals to a deeply disillusioned 69-year-old Eugène Ysaÿe.

* * *

When – at the age of eighty – Casals decided to marry the twenty-year-old Marta Montañez, his doctor attempted to warn him of the grave consequences this might present for his health.

'It could even', he suggested, 'be a matter of life or death.'

The lively octogenarian sucked slowly on his pipe, reflecting on the dilemma, before replying: 'Well, I look at it this way. If she dies, she dies.'

* * *

In 1958, Casals returned to Prades physically exhausted from the strain of concert-giving and travelling.
After greeting him his friend René Puig, the phy-
sician, suggested that a slight slackening of the pace
might not come amiss and that a short holiday, with
complete rest, would be even more advisable.

'No!' countered Casals. 'To stop, to retire even for a
short time, is to begin to die.'

* * *

By the time Casals had reached his nineties, nearly
every interviewer would ask him to divulge the secret
of his longevity. His favourite answer to this was:
'The opportunity life gives me to draw a bow across
my cello every day.' Once, however, when asked the
inevitable question on television, he rounded on his
interrogator and – looking more like a man in his
sixties – cried out: 'I *live*! Very few people live.'

* * *

In Casals's later years, Marta used to carry an oxygen mask with her in case of emergencies. Casals never used the oxygen himself at concerts, although it was required more than once to revive elderly ladies overcome with emotion. However, at one performance of his oratorio *El Pessebre* in Central America, the orchestra was mediocre and the chorus – mostly local singers – was willing but dreadful. Alexander Schneider had done his best in rehearsal, and at the concert Casals, then nearly ninety-two, conducted demonically to try and create an illusion of splendour from the chaos. As the 'performance' proceeded, Marta noticed with horror that her husband's face was growing redder and redder – not through fatigue, as she thought, but fury.

Quickly, she shoved the astonished Schneider on stage to conduct the rest of the performance. Dragging her husband off, she clamped the oxygen mask over his face while Casals slumped back in his chair, groaning repeatedly every time he heard a wrong note.

* * *

'I practise constantly – as if I am going to live for a thousand years,' said the 95-year-old Casals.

*   *   *

'My word!' exclaimed a visiting doctor, having just watched the 95-year-old Casals rehearse a Haydn symphony, 'your energy this morning was more like a man of forty.'

'*Twenty*!' snapped Casals, his eyes widening. 'I may be an old man, but in music I am very young.'

*   *   *

'It is true I am no longer very young,' said Casals, aged ninety-six:

> For example, I am not as young as I was at ninety. Age is relative. If we continue to work and absorb the beauties of the world around us, we shall soon realise that an increasing number of years do not have to mean we are growing old. Now that I am in my nineties I feel some things more intensely than when

I was a young man – and I find life more and more fascinating every day.

*   *   *

When asked, at ninety-six, whether he still practised, Casals replied: 'Naturally I go on playing and practising – and I would continue to do so even if I lived for another hundred years. How could I desert my oldest friend – the cello?'

*   *   *

In June 1973, four months before his death, the 97-year-old Casals addressed a large crowd at a concert in Central Park:

I am perhaps the oldest musician in the world. I am an old man, but in many ways I am a very young man. And this is what I want you to be! *Young, young* all your life, and to say things to the world that are true. Goodness, love – this is the real world. Let us have love, love and peace.

On Stradivarius

'I have never been tempted to own a Stradivarius. In my opinion these superb instruments have too much personality; when I play on one, I can never forget that I have a Stradivarius in my hands – and it disturbs me considerably.'

*   *   *

When asked why he chose not to play on a Stradivarius, Casals replied: 'I like to hear Casals.'

On his pipes

Casals was well known to be passionately fond of his pipe and – away from his cello – was rarely seen without it. This worried some of his friends and colleagues, but their warnings were to no avail. When challenged on how much he smoked, he would reply: 'As much as possible.'

* * *

One interviewer commented: 'I understand the London Symphony Orchestra presented you with a wonderful collection of English pipes?'

'Yes,' Casals replied, a wicked smile creeping over his face at the memory:

I had been to see the doctor earlier that day, as I wasn't feeling well, and he told me I had to stop smoking. I was deeply affected by this gloomy prospect when, the very same evening, the London Symphony Orchestra sent me a magnificent collection of English pipes as a present! What was I to do but use them?

On education

'I have an idea – a plan – for the education of children. I have spoken about this to many important people and they say: "It is so simple, yet we have
never thought of it." It is this: as soon as a child is
old enough to understand the meaning of a word, he
should be told that this word represents a miracle.
When we speak of the eye, we should explain what a
miracle it is to be able to see. We should explain what
a miracle it is to be able to speak. What a marvel
are our hands! When the wonder of each word has
been made clear, then every child should be taught
to realise: "*I* am a miracle – and *he* is also a miracle.
Therefore, *I cannot kill him – and he cannot kill me.*"
Only in this way can we rid ourselves of the impulse

of war. At school, they teach that two and two make four. That is not what life is all about.'

On retirement

'Retire? The idea is inconceivable to me. I don't believe in retirement for anyone in my type of work – not if the spirit remains. My work is my life. I cannot think of one without the other. To "retire" means to me to die. The man who works and is not bored is never old. Work and interest in worthwhile things are the best medicine for age. Each day I am reborn. Each day I begin again.'

On work

'There is, of course, no substitute for work. I myself practise constantly, as I have done all my life. I have been told I play the cello with the ease of a bird flying. I do not know with how much effort a bird learns to fly, but I do know what effort has gone into my cello. What seems ease of performance comes only from the greatest labour.'

*   *   *

'One's work should be a salute to life.'

Acknowledgements

Grateful acknowledgements and thanks are due to the many friends and colleagues whose tales of 'the little Catalan maestro' prompted this book.

I am indebted to the following for their kind permission to use excerpts from their publications: Hutchinson Publishing Group for *Royal Philharmonic* by Robert Elkin and *Conversations with Casals* by J. Ma. Corredor; Heinemann for *Casals and the Art of Interpretation* by David Blum and *Paul Tortelier: A Self Portrait*, also by David Blum; Thames Publishing Limited for *Blow by Blow* by Archie Camden; Hamish Hamilton Limited for *At the Piano* by Ivor Newton and *Myra Hess – A Portrait* by Marian McKenna; Lady Trudy Bliss for *As I Remember* by Sir Arthur Bliss; Margaret Campbell for *The Great Violinists*; Jonathan

Cape for *My Young Years* by Artur Rubinstein; EMI Records Limited for *The Art of Pablo Casals* (© Juan Manuel Puente, 1976, English translations © Geoffrey Watkins 1976, from *The Art of Pablo Casals*, the HMV Treasury Series, RLS 723–3 LPs plus booklet, by permission of the author and translator and EMI Records Limited); Macmillan Publishing Company for *Conversations with Igor Oistrakh* by Viktor Jusefovich (reprinted by permission of Macmillan Publishing Company, from *Conversations with Igor Oistrakh* by Viktor Jusefovich, originally published by Cassell & Co Ltd); W. W. Norton and Company Inc for extracts from p. 14, p. 68 and p. 169 of *Pablo Casals, A Life* by Lillian Littlehales (by permission of W. W. Norton and Company Inc, © 1929, 1948) and for extracts from *Harold Bauer, His Book* by Harold Bauer (by permission of W. W. Norton and Company Inc, © 1948, © 1976 Wynn Bauer). Special thanks are necessary to A. M. Heath for their kind permission to use material from H. L. Kirk's masterly and authoritative biography *Pablo Casals* and Simon Schuster for their kind permission to use material from Albert E. Kahn's inspirational volume *Joys and Sorrows*.

About the editor

Julian Lloyd Webber is one of the leading musi-cians of our time. As a solo cellist, he played with the world's greatest orchestras in the world's most famous concert halls and recorded with musical legends including Yehudi Menuhin, Georg Solti, Stéphane Grappelli and Elton John. His recording of Elgar's Cello Concerto won the Classical Brit Award in 1978, and his album *Variations* won a gold disc within five weeks of its release. In 2008, Julian found-ed the UK government's In Harmony programme, which facilitates access to music for children from less-privileged backgrounds. Julian was the only clas-sical musician chosen to play at the closing ceremony of the 2012 Summer Olympic Games.

In 2014, a neck injury reduced the power of his

bowing arm, forcing his retirement as a cellist. The following year, he was appointed principal of the Royal Birmingham Conservatoire, a role which he held for five years. He continues to support young musicians through regular television and radio programmes on rising classical stars.

Julian is a lifelong Leyton Orient supporter, and he was the London Underground's first official busker.